73

Cut to Bloom

℥

by Arhm Choi Wild

Write Bloody Publishing

writebloody.com

First edition.
ISBN: 978-1949342215

Cover Design by Zoe Norvell
Interior Layout by Winona León
Edited by Chelsea Bayouth and Derrick C. Brown
Proofread by Sun Yung Shin
Author Photo by Sy Klipsch-Abudu

Type set in Bergamo from www.theleagueofmoveabletype.com

Printed in the USA

Write Bloody Publishing
Los Angeles, CA

Support Independent Presses
writebloody.com

for Umma, who made this book (everything) possible

Cut to Bloom

CUT TO BLOOM

한/*han*

rogue bouquet

and I ask myself and you, which of our visions will claim us

—Adrienne Rich

한/*han*

INHERITANCE

If I speak now
I deny generations
of mouths politely closed
or pummeled smooth,
hiding folds of cash
until bruises crowd
and we finally say
enough.

In our family I am the first
American. What choice
is there but to grunt and pry
at what has been slammed closed,
to love open like sunflowers
following the sun
trusting to be fed
not burned?

To be the first
means to salvage.
What choice is there
but to peel off the flies
caught on my sticky tongue?

THE ARIA THIEF: PART I

My father was the first man
she ever kissed.

He showed up in Vienna
where she had already found
what she loved,
warming up her throat
with scales that cut
the grip of cold.

Back then, she ate only rice
and seaweed to save
for songbooks and lessons.
He ate in small hotels
walking the city
every day, listening
for the soprano
he'd heard only once
back in Seoul.

Every morning
he bought flowers
that wilted to bent necks
by the afternoon roast.

He found her at lunch
walking between classes,
right before the bouquet
turned away. How could she

refuse a man
who searched for her
in a country
that didn't understand
his questions?

THE ARIA THIEF: PART II

Back home
he yanks Mama's mouth
round into screams

burns her vocal cords,
strands her nightingales
in the winter
of his cold cocktail gins

makes them croak
out a song
when he bends
her neck

the skin
gathered
in his fist.

Mother's silence
when he holds a knife
to her stomach.
Mother's silence
when the cops leave
and the phone rings,
blaming her
for his rage.

If I fail my mouth
this story plays again—
can't close
closet
cease.

I must become the skip
in the disk, the fracture
that makes the needle jump,
land on anything
but this.

Ever the Pests

Our pants pooled at our ankles,
Mo & I study Appa in the mirror,
a fly swatter gripped in his hands.

During the summer,
it lies by the kitchen table
to be snatched up quick.

I watch my sister's eyes widen
and collapse like the ribs of a fish
as the plastic swishes
in the air. I don't remember
what we did wrong.

After, he walks out
leaving the swatter on the floor
where we can see it.

We tiptoe up to grab
the salve in the cabinet
and take turns
smoothing it on legs
red with the promise of welts.

That summer, we keep
all windows closed
to lock out anything
that flies.

FOOL ME ONCE

His knees buckle
in a drunk pigeon walk,
knocking chairs
around, catching
himself loudly
on the table.

Mom hides
in side room
nursing baby sister
though her breasts
have seized.

I tried to lock
the door faster
but he's inside

pulling us down the hall,
saying *Only terrible daughters*
aren't happy to see their dad.

He holds our shoulders tight.
We make our faces pebbles
that fervent thumbs
rub smooth.
Call the cops again
and I'll kill you.

I dial the phone while I pretend
to pee. We hid one in the blanket closet
just for nights like this.

He leaves before the cops come,
the river of him slashing sideways

Mama in side room,
Baby still hungry,
Mo & I
sucking back
into our mouths
the air
we let him take.

VUL/NER/A/BLE: /ˈvəln(ə)rəbəl/
after A. Van Jordan

17ᵗʰ century Latin *to wound*. trunk without branches. pits of plums. empty couches. five cups of coffee lost in a dark city with no shoes and no number to call. empty discount food bins. counting cookies at the party again, a ready ziploc thrust deep into a pocket. holding up the rearview mirror with my hand instead of glue. a nightingale with sunburn. Mother staring at a spot above Mo's face while we hide under the porch, waiting for the cops to come. to close the door quiet like a bent rose. an iris blooming under a sky that does not notice.

Fear Changes the Taste of Breast Milk Like an Animal's Violent Slaughter Spoils Its Meat

The day after,
the chairs are back in place

the handprints on the table
and our faces
wiped clean.

Still Baby protests,
doesn't take Mom's breast
though she pleas
then prays
then pumps to try the bottle.

Mo & I are thirteen and ten,
young enough
to make a game
of survival.

We take a bottle each
and mimic for Baby
how to feed

get to be heroes
when she giggles,
reaches for milk
of her own.

We dart our eyes
to Mom to see
if it's our turn
to be held.

THE LAST BRUISE

Whenever my mother takes
the stairs, I remember
how he pushed her down

arms abandoning her face
to circle her pregnant belly,
cracking like a watermelon
at my feet.

Three months later,
Mom moves us home
from the shelter,
restraining order circling
like an electric fence

my newest job
to translate
the welfare stamps
and mix the formula

while Umma sells tupperware
then knives, tries hosting
wealthy students from Korea.
She watches their plates
for leftover chicken or rice,
never sitting down
for a meal, choosing instead

the certainty of hunger
to be a woman unowned.

An Empty Home, a Playground

Monkey! I yell as Baby climbs onto the plastic cabinet handles. She giggles when they break and plops down in her pink pants and matching shirt. I carry her upside down to the living room, saying things she doesn't get yet, like *expensive & blame & Mama's wrath.*

At age two Baby is textbook terrible, the Sherlock Holmes to every baby-proofed lock, tupperware bent out of drawers, splayed like a plastic massacre. We clean up the same war again and again in the same spot he kicked Mom's stomach. We were shocked when Baby was born perfect.

After we run away and come back, clean up the freezer bags of chicken and beer bottles left like bowling pins, we roll out dumplings on the counter that Mom sells for fifty cents each, her bruises now the green of an old scallion flashing in and out of the raw egg, ground beef, and carrots.

We sit Baby on the counter, the only one who can make us laugh, with a spoon or broken wrapper to play with while we pack, seal, and fry, one ear pricked for a car, his return, one ear on Baby banging away with her spoon.

On Mo's 18th birthday, the same counter is lined with handles of no-name liquor in a kitchen absent of a mother trying to not drown in all that she doesn't want.

Lavender streamers hang from the cabinet handles Mo replaced before Mom noticed, one wrapped around Baby's middle, streaming behind her as she hides under a dresser or is tossed through the air to a peal of giggles.

Baby is clasping a sippy cup like everyone else, the kitchen still her domain until someone, laughing, slips vodka into her cup and Baby, too old now to be losing her balance, lolls her head too far back, and then there is Mo with a trembling boy blown against the wall, hurling him into the yard and whipping his shoes after him, locking the door so hard it shakes.

I take Baby to my bed so I can watch her from the roof while I smoke cigarettes, one eye on the bed, the other on the road.

THE MEMORY KEEPER

Umma doesn't ask how I have this photo:
I am curled inside a basket of books
with room enough to swing
the spoon I hold.

We left Korea in '92
without knowing
we wouldn't return;
all photos of Mom's parents, all
the happy ones of Appa
left behind.

In 7th grade Mo & I went back,
the year I discovered Tupac and played
his *Greatest Hits* on repeat.

Everything in our old room was left exactly the same—
our doll house in the closet,
umbrella stand full of my baseball bats
and plastic guns innocent with dust.

I am listening to "Dear Mama" when my older sister walks in,
checking down the hallway before closing the door.
Look, she says, quiet, pulling a pile
from under her shirt.

She has the one of her and me in a field of flowers,
Mom in huge '90s glasses holding me as I reach
for the camera, Mo at her first violin recital, us again
at the pool, floating like baby otters
with green swim caps on.

Let's bring them back, she says. *Mom will be so happy
to see these*, and she pulls out a photograph
of our grandmother, the one before she got cancer,
the one they used at the funeral, the one thing
Umma wished she hadn't left behind.

When my father finds out the photos are missing,
he grabs Mo by her long thick braid
and shoves her against the wall. She crumples
like how the ash of a cigarette holds its shape
until it submits to the earth.

I am still listening to Tupac when she sneaks
back into Appa's room while he is out
for another six-pack.

When we get home two weeks later,
the bruises on her face and back
have disappeared. She uses all
the money she saved
and takes the photos to the shop
to get them framed.

There's the one
where she's dancing in *Swan Lake*,
the one we are being lizards
on the couch, the one where her hair
is in a braid again and she is holding me,
her thin arm wrapped
around my shoulders

like she is the only one
who can trick the world
into bringing me what is mine.

LATCHKEY CORONATION

When your sister leaves for college
you can't ask her to stay

so you let yourself cry only
on the drive to the dorm room
and not when you close the door
or walk in again because Mo
calls you back, your relief so palpable
you could tuck it under
the single framed bed.

You should be celebrating,
now the new crowned king
of the twenty dollars left
under the telephone for dinner, the choice
between pizza or cigarettes, gas
or weed entirely your own. You avoid
her room for weeks until
you can pretend
it's always been this way,

driving alone to pick up little sister,
bringing her to camp,
filling out the forms,
packing her lunch and adding
little notes so at least one of you

will wait to be picked up from school
without worrying she'd been forgotten,
will know hunger is a pebble to collect
then return to the shore of the lake,
will know if she makes a mistake
she will have someone
to apologize to, will know
how easy it is to make
people bend for her,
then later, perhaps
what it's like to be the one
who falls to her knees.

CIRCLE TALK
for Umma

How do I know who I love when you can't
say *this is me*? What is the point
of knowing English if all I can draw
are circles when you draw lines?
How can I draw lines to a past if it is hidden
by a screen of broken moths? If you
are a past hidden by broken moths, what will I call
my children? What will they call you? A cloud? A piece of wheat?
If you are a cloud, and I am a piece of wheat,
how do moths find their way in the dark?
If we ever found our way through the dark
to touch each other's mouths with small hands,
how will we make up for lost time?
If I have your small hands, how do our mouths fail us again?

THE FORGOTTEN WAR[1]

i.
my grandfather was a soldier in a war
where only white men   could be heroes
and my people   the herd   to be saved

three million   Korean civilians   killed
pocketed   like coins   for democracy

which is to say
he was born   a pawn
born   to forget   who pulled
the trigger

---

1 *The Korean War is often referred to as "the Forgotten War" because of its absence from U.S. public attention.*

ii.
Grandmother never talks[2]
about her childhood and hoards
everything, cabinets of ketchup
and SPAM, reused toilet paper
drying on the sink's edge,
teaching us to pick up each
grain of rice, eyeing the outskirts
of our plates, never talking
about the Korean pried out
like teeth, born to forget
the name her mother called her,
foraging instead for words
like *hunger* and *please*.

---

2 *Japan colonized Korea for 35 years before the Korean War, forcing everyone to take on Japanese names and speak only in Japanese. Secretary Taft sanctioned this occupation as long as Japan agreed the U.S. could continue to control the Philippines.*

iii.

what is a plea   in the language
of men   collecting
a half million
Comfort Women[3], many
only twelve, most dying
from multiple   stds

what does a person deserve
after years   of days
like that

surely more   than the dollar

the few hundred   out of thousands
of Comfort Women   to remain
received   as reparations

---

3 *Hundreds of thousands of women were forced into sexual servitude by the Japanese military until the end of World War II. American military personnel continued to visit the "comfort stations" until they were closed in 1946.*

iv.
the word *han* in Korean means to celebrate your survival
in silence, knowing you weren't the only one to pay the price

means seeing there is less than a grain of rice
and still setting the table

means that when they steal your shovel,
use your hands and plant the garden anyway.

v.
it took my aunt years
to divorce her abusive husband,
choosing a bruised neck
over an empty mouth.
she now works at a 7-eleven,
borrows money from my mom
for her daughter's wedding,
tries to still her voice
into a frozen lake when she calls,
her choice to leave her husband
the same as leaving the church,
single mothers being outcasts
in Korea, which is to say
being a woman
is the loneliest thing
if you are trying
to survive.

vi.
my mother, in trying to survive
made us speak english at home
knowing we wouldn't be able
to defend the family
in our mother tongue.

she says the word *han*
is my birthright,
something every Korean owns

but who am I to define
this prized ruin,
this fertile ash

far from fluent,
saying *thank you*
like a foreigner
craving to fit
into the language
of home and memory, split
from the homeland
we wouldn't
have survived,
queer and single-mothered,
split   from holding
each other's words
in our mouths
like our own, missing
what was never ours.

yet I am this fool
coming to praise
if not love
the fracture,
knowing it has allowed us
to choose   if not forget

and my mother can be more
than a survivor
and I can be more
than a daughter
who was trained
to never ask   for more.

LEGEND

Like a good Korean woman
you take whatever is passed:
a cup of rain, an empty fist,
a story without a mouth.

But every truth has something
that makes you believe in a lie.
Every mother has a gift
she never meant to give.

Is it true Grandfather left you
on your aunt's porch one winter,
holding a small note
instructing you to wait?

Two weeks became two months,
two years, a decade?

I was twenty-one the first time
you told me this, one bright morning
with sparrows tossing in the air.

Remember how you stopped
halfway, started cooking
as if this hunger
could be filled?

Is it true you watched
him walk away? Is it true
that when he picked you up
ten years later, you walked back
into his arms, not the girl he left
but a woman with tough hands?

Is it true that learning
how to feed yourself
what the men
have failed to provide
is the gift you wished
you never had to give?

A PIECE OF THE HEIRLOOM

Not even a photo, or a letter.
Umma inherited only one thing
from her parents: a painting of two people
walking down a country road
by a field that begs for rain.

Halmoni yanks at the frame
while Mo & I drag it
to the cab. She let the taunting sun
strip it white, the black of the road
the only thing left.

Mo is the only one with enough Korean to say
There is only so much we can let you take.

Grandma feigns to clutch her chest,
tears like stickers quickly placed
on her cheeks.

I refuse to look back as we drive away
but still, even people I despise
can make me soften like a peach
at the bottom of a bag.

Back in the hotel room, Umma stares at the painting,
closes her eyes, remembers what the sun took.

We leave it here, she says, and walks out in hotel slippers.

The Family Business: Iris Cleaners

Some people have problems
distinguishing a dry cleaner
from a laundromat

but Mother wasn't meant
to make her mouth a seam,
wash blood out of sheets
or the piss of an aging man every week
and my belly is too full and my car is too new
for us to forget, so I will tell you

a laundromat is the one with the quarters
and the dry cleaner is where workers
finger spots of wine like bruises.

Mr. Washington never fails
to ask for a discount
no matter how hard it is
to get his chocolate stains out.

Mr. Francis always brings clothes
with foundation and eye shadow
in the fabric of his collar,
tells me of drunken nights;
it's not hard to figure out
why he winks.

Ms. Miller walks in with one ear
punched by a steel rod,
other lobe, four rings.

One day I ask her
what it symbolized and she replies
It's a statement I make
so people will realize that a woman
can decorate her body
without being flooded with questions.

She quizzes me on what I unlearned about the patriarchy
in the past week and loves when Mom has her clothes ready
before she's in the door.

Lately in these summer days
Mom comes home braised with heat rash
because if lucky, it's only twenty degrees hotter inside than out.

We could make a separate fortune
if she chose not to play good Samaritan
but she returns every quarter found in pockets.

Chemical scents follow her like a conscience
and her hands stay constant with cracks
no lotion can recover. She used to count on fingers
the shirts and sweaters soaked with sweat and blood
she washed to pay my cell phone bill.

I thought she was just imposing guilt
till when working one day
a man with a snarl slick with spit
full of English words Mom didn't know,
but felt, threatened to sue for the stubborn
spot of wine he let sit for weeks,
the jacket he left at a hotel but blamed us
for losing, surely unable to defend
ourselves, Mom barely
five feet tall, too polite
to wipe his spit off her chin.

Two weeks later, a brick without a head
to fly toward breaks the window in the middle
of the night and we can no longer
be proud without looking
out of place. Mom doesn't call
the cops and pays extra
to fix the window by Monday.

If I save myself in time
I won't be lost in this business
of erasing everything

so I need you to remember
a laundromat is the one with the quarters
and the dry cleaner
is where my mother
will give them back to you
if you leave them
in your pockets.

13ᵀᴴ ANNIVERSARY

She walks in alone after hours, all the machines quiet though she can't hate them today. The dry-cleaning tank is square and tall so she must stand on tip-toes to run her parched hands along the top, muttering old Korean in neat strands of sound. A piece of skin flakes off when she rubs the metal of the shirt press. The spot with burn stains, she circles twice. Every year she comes to thank the machines that break on her—thank them for the days they clean hundreds of sweaters and baskets of shirts, thank them for feeding her daughters though not her heart. She bows to the sheet metal too bent to reflect, creaks to her knees and rests her forehead on top of her hands in the ritual she has been handed down from her own mother, who will never know that her opera singer has come to worship the machines.

rogue bouquet

*Dedicating your life to understanding yourself
can be its own form of protest.*

—Samra Habib

ALLEGIANCE

The taxi driver thinks none of us speak English
when I, sleepy, check out musing only
of sweet things, like the cheek of a persimmon
and tea below the Mason-Dixon.

Umma is silent, embarrassed
by her accent, thick
as beer or regret.

The driver is impatient until my sister
tells him to take us from Detroit to suburbia
where I bought cigarettes at fifteen
with a fake ID because people there think
all Asians look the same.

We get out at the house we grew up in
where we are Mom's 애들 at Thanksgiving
even though we talk in slang
picked up at the corner store.
I say *dope*, she hears drugs.
I say *sick*, she calls the doctor.

Still, she has our favorite foods waiting:
식혜, blackberries, 만두,
raisin bread from the famous
neighborhood bakery.
She always forgets it's not the raisins I like
but the taste of home I miss.

If I could speak Korean well enough,
I would tell her how relieved I am
to finally find articles where race
is no longer just black and white
and I can write in the margins
this is like my family.

Instead we discuss only simple things
and she smiles like the bottom
of a plain bowl, desperate
to curl up around whatever
I throw in. Sometimes I say really odd shit
just to see if she gets me. Again, the smile.

I know she grew up missing her father
but I don't know his name.
I know she writes poetry
but I don't know
what she calls herself
in the dark.

Mom quietly prepares
kimchi on white plates
while my sisters and I catch up.

We're in charge of the mashed potatoes
and this year, they are delicious.
We have finally
stored enough salt
and butter in our blood
to make the dishes strut
though it's not
what I crave when I am sick
or hungry for laughter.

The familiar 떡국 and steaming 갈비
make half the room smell
of Confucian traditions we grumpily perform

while the turkey smells
of rich conversations
we feel guilty for having in English.

Umma arms us with gum
as we drive back to cities
that take pictures of us
for multicultural week.
She says 몸조심해
and I wonder how to say *for you, always*

but my throat has always betrayed me.
I just nod and walk out the door.

What It Takes to Call a Place Your Own

In North Carolina the trunks of cherry trees
grow extra wide. I lounge
on branches and pull the blooms
to my face in the peak of spring.

The dirt in Asheville
glitters in the sun,
mica inside every piece,
in gutters, on porches

even in my hand
when I shove fistfuls
into my mouth

wanting to think
I too am made of blue mountains
that make the sky shine.

At the restaurant I gnaw
my barbecue ribs
like everyone else,
people gawking
surprised to see me
this far south.

A veteran in the street
says he killed my people
in the Korean War,
like this is something
to share over drinks

but even now, hundreds of miles
away in New York City, I dream
of hemlocks leading me back
to the river's edge
where I let her see
what I hide
inside my pockets.

If only none of this mattered,
I could follow my partner
back South, instead of staying here
where there is no square of earth
to call my own

but I can call it home
without being asked
how I learned to speak English so well.

TAKE WHAT YOU CAN

The broken piano of the train tracks
tells me I'm in New York,
the city that carts people
like mobile homes across itself.

A friend told me last night
that being uncomfortable
will help me find my voice, as if
I could squeeze it out
of a melon, skim
it off the soup, bloody
a tomato trying to get
at my seeds.

I no longer have to go
to motherlands to search
for the culture I have lost,
lost like caps to pens
or misplaced coasters
when the tea is burning my hand
and I'm surrounded by antique wood.

Walking around Koreatown
I run my hands along my face
and find it is still mine.

I don't feel like I'm home,
but if I wanted, I could disappear
into the crowd.

At What Cost

Gay people don't exist in Seoul, South Korea

don't get dragged behind cars or dream of lynching ropes,
don't scream underneath burning houses or the fire hose,
don't orgasm, don't lose their teeth and then their dentures,
don't forget their tampons, don't make love in the bathtub
and again on the floor because they have fallen in love twice
that day, don't run a finger over a cheek, wake up for a second
to pull themselves closer, don't pick up a hammer to bust in
an idea, don't dream, don't fuck, don't say *I love you*, don't dream
of fucking to say *I love you*, don't skip brushing their teeth,
don't try to stay friends with their exes
because in Korea, gay people don't exist.

A group of boys move off the sidewalk
to give me space. Boy on left
with his hand in back pocket
of boy in the middle who reaches over
to brush the hair out of other boy's eyes,
all three laughing, all free
to show love without risk
in this homo-blind world.

I walk past the boys, duck into a food stall.
It's cold so I ask for the hot fish soup,
look up from styrofoam cup
to see a woman with her hand on the thigh of a friend,
a finger going up to wipe off a cheek and kiss it,
all as part of the conversation
easy like punctuation marks, regular like periods.

My family is no different.
My aunt walks down the street holding my hand
as the glamorous gingko trees stand guard.
Later that day, another relative talks to me
with the help of her hand on my knee
because I can't speak deep in Korean.

They touch me with no idea
of what a woman's hands have meant to me,
how they curl around a coffee cup
or flip through a book have turned me on.
In my motherland,
I don't dare ask how to say *gay*
because I'm afraid
the word doesn't exist.

At what cost
can men get the affection
they need from other men?

At what cost do I turn
all past lovers into men, Sarah
into Samuel, Megan into Mark?

At what cost
will I come out to my family
and have them still see me?

It is for the cost of loving this country,
of finally feeling like I fit in
like I have found the people
to whom I belong.

Gay people don't exist in Korea
and I am holding back a tongue
that could break this mirage
because seeing men not afraid to hold hands
and fix each other's ties is too beautiful —
beautiful like a kiss in the naked soft of morning,
beautiful like a mother
welcoming her daughter home.

WHEN I VISIT MY FATHER FOR THE LAST TIME: PART I

He is riding down the ribbon of road
with his head out the sunroof window.
The wind pushing his face, his lungs bloom.

At fifty-three he's getting his first lesson in flying,
shirt collar whipping around his neck,
mouth half open like a loose fist.

His Volvo is packed with cigarettes,
one bottle of water. I wonder
what his attention tastes like
and shyly lick the rim.

He has been stutter-stop-
and-go since I've been here.
He taught me how drunk drivers
like pounding the gas
along with their wife

but I'm in the driver's seat now
with all this reckless speed at my feet.
If I wanted, I could drive into the guardrail,
snap his neck, send it careening
down the mountain.

Instead, I reach to hold his hand,
hardened by twisting cheap lids
from bottles of vodka.

Every three months, the skin on the body
is entirely remade. In three months
I will have never touched him.

WHEN I VISIT MY FATHER FOR THE LAST TIME: PART II

Halmoni pretends at forgetting
when we ask about her son,
ten minutes late so still only a photo
to the youngest of us who has yet to meet him.

Talking with this woman
is like gulping SPAM with no time
to breathe. She still thinks the divorce
is Umma's fault, says she complains
too much. The retorts I silence
twist my lips into a melted rim.

I sit on the edge of the couch with arms crossed
when she tries to capture us in a photo. Baby sister smiles
because she still has chances to give.

An hour now, and Appa still hasn't shown.
Baby wonders what time stubble grows back on a face,
what men smell like when late and nervous.

Thirty minutes later
I let fury cut a way to the door.

UNDONE

You slip on the water in the kitchen, wet hair
from the shower turning the ground shiny,
treacherous. Is this what heartbreak is,
to break a hip or wrist in the war
of your own making? You can sing
yourself empty until the morning comes,
break all your fingers to make
a new hand. But this collar bone
wasn't meant for this neck. Send it back
to be the ring around the moon. No one
dies from loss unless you take the knife and flay
the veins on your thigh like the belly of a small fish
and push deeper, until you really do forget
how your hands can't hold anything, even your own blood.

My Father Is Kneeling in the Dark

The last hour
of his birthday
is spent staring
at three shot glasses
empty before him.

His daughters
are in the country
he brought them to
and left them in,
busy cooking dinner, kissing
their partners, picking
up socks.

There is no prescription
for forgetting
so they all do it differently,
daughters looking away
from the calendar,
Father trying not
to glance at the phone
or the bottle smashed
against the wall
in his cigarette-strewn
apartment. At some point

absence becomes
a well, dipped into
until it's a part
of everything,

even the vials of his cologne
you break in your hands

so your blood turns fragrant
and betrays you
by smelling beautiful.

A Scavenger's Prayer

I stand in the ocean, the wind dark
against my face and salty hair. Never
have I been stranded by the sunrise,
the black slowly turning to grey
and now come the pelicans.

I think of all the women before me
who have come to be washed clean by the water.
I too will trail my fingers along the surface
making my own small waves. I too will stay
in the salt until I have emptied
my blood of his face

until I can believe in more
than how hard I quake,

come to love the sound
of cracking open

just like when the waves come

and the scavengers of the sea

break into flight.

FOR THE SAKE OF LIGHT

I am a mess of egg,
pieces of shell
in sheets
like lips
peeled in winter.

In one myth, the crow
is burned black
when bringing fire
down from the gods.

I am scared
of my burnt wings

but if I choose

to be shell
and lip
and mess

there is no need
to fear the fire
whispering
along my bones.

WHATEVER IT IS WE HAVE FAITH IN

It is finally springtime.
Whenever the ground shakes

I close my eyes
like my daddy taught me.

I could fall madly for the woman
in my bed and I'm trying to stay here

on this soft shoulder, this robin
egg room with windows open

trying to ignore my instinct to hug
my knees and stuff my ears.

My lover's song
swears to not leave me

in fractures but
I want

to love
so open

I could break.
While lilacs hum, and cherries burst

and the dark gets left behind,
I lift my hands up to her face

widen my neck to her teeth,
let someone in

who could make me lose
the name

to all my gods.

STORY OF MY NAME
after María Luisa Arroyo

I.
아름아, Umma calls.
I'm talking to my partner on Mama's couch,
telling her the same things I've been saying all my life:
Korean doesn't have a *r* sound, it's more like *r-d-l*
all smushed together, not a roll like in Spanish.

I see this woman I love mimicking the sounds of it,
her lips turning the corner of the page, almost.

Rice is luck in Korean and 아름 means lots of it.
It also means *big hug*, as in the armful of flowers
that hides my face and too, an adjective, meaning beautiful—

예쁘다
아름
아름답다

II.
My parents had just moved
to Detroit and couldn't yet
make English work
for them. Hours
before I was born
they asked the doctors
how to spell my name,
honoring their suggestion letter
by letter, bowing low
before the true Americans.
Even then.

III.
There is a market
in Korea's corner of Manhattan
that is also called 아름.

Sometimes I walk by without a grocery list
to see myself outside
the crude answer of my body

but I don't want to explain this
to every person I meet
so I let English conquer my tongue,
say *Hi, my name is Autumn*

and people will say *Your name is beautiful*,
thinking of trees not afraid
of biting their own
apple foliage.

IV.
In Korean *autumn* is 가을
which does not hold the time I fell
down the steps of the Jefferson Memorial
or the first time I bit someone else's lip.

I catch myself wishing
people wouldn't try to say it right
like *Arham* or *Arum*,

let me deny
my parent's immigrant ignorance
and the culture that lets
me be luck and hug and beautiful.

Autumn is how I make
reservations for tables and doctors.

Autumn gives me a mask
like everyone else,

so why am I falling more in love
with the woman listening so intently
to the way my mother commands my name?

I must convince her it's ok
if she doesn't say it right

but I must admit
I am so happy when she does.

UNTIL I'M READY

You kiss the grapefruit
and tuck it back
into your bag. I've stopped asking
what makes you laugh,
rounding off your lips
like grapes devoured
by the birds. The train car
is full of them. I sit next to you,
shy, hiding with my jacket
your hand I hold. I scan
the car for the wrong glare,
a curled fist. You don't notice
the snarl of the 언니 walking past,
the shocked face of the 오빠,
and to kiss you means to ignore
the hard heels, the heavy keys.

This is the one city I've lived in
that will allow me to marry
and also hear people say my name
with ease. I've lived my whole life
being called something wrong
until this city that says *Arhm*
without stumbling, *Arhm*
without a second look.

Koreatown sits on 32nd street
between Broadway and 5th,
one block that is home and blood
but blood is not
a dyke, doesn't trip
over my teeth,
so I ask you to wait
to kiss me until we are across
the street. If another Korean
gives me the same look
as the woman on the train,

I would turn into a clock
without the sun, a thirst
without a cup, so you kiss
the grapefruit instead and laugh
and people turn their heads
anyway.

Compromise

I'm walking with my partner in Brooklyn,
the scent of spring almost but not yet,
the feel of her hand familiar but not yet

when a man slides up next to us and whispers
If you come home with me tonight
I'll make both of you happy.

It is 2019, in New York City
and we are grown women
with cell phones and keys to hold in our fists
so this man should get punched or arrested
but we just laugh nervously,
walk a little faster when he calls after us
Wait, we can just go to my car.

I remember the time
we were chased out of the park
by a group of five men
for sitting too close together in the grass
eating our sandwiches

and all we could do was call the cops
knowing they would do nothing,
seeing their smirks as they take
our names and yes, we can get married,
buy a house, send our children to school

if we're constantly on the lookout
if we're willing to let go of each other's hands
if all we defend ourselves with
is our nervous laughter.

FALL FOR HER

Fuck it. Fill your hands
with her though you tremble,
the daisy outside your door
stuck between bending
beneath the wind
and rising from the ground.

Fickle inheritance. You learned
the romance of being unseen. The moment
you should move from chair to under table,
just when your father turns away, just
before he picks up the hammer
and wonders where to throw.

When she looks at you,
holds out a hand, does she realize
what she is asking?
Does she see how deeply
your memories of him
wrap around your spine
with their greedy long limbs,
claiming tailbone, your tongue,
your skin too sweaty to grasp?

She is a bullet not meant to hurt you.
A bullet wanting to shine its face with your blood
in order to know the way you move. Intimacy
is its own kind of death; learning to say *yes*
to this ash, to say *enter*
as easily as you say *hide*, how to still
while the bullet comes.

Fall or stay perched inside the small cage
of your teeth. Fall or agree to a life of being half,
never more than a hand
that knows to tighten in a fist
or unleash a sting
and you've lost your chance to forget
you're the daughter
of a violent man.

The Gift You Make of Patience

The curve of a poppy
is the closest thing
to the curve of your head
you lay on my lap,
letting me smooth
your hair with hands I want
to let you bite and trust
my skin is wise enough to not
make fools of your teeth.

You call me up
though the dark earth says *stay*.
You call me in
though it's still shattered there
and you take my hands
to run over the surface that rushes
with the good blood. How do you see
such good in me
when I have forgotten
my face? I closed a door
and you were suddenly
in the room. I opened
a window and heard
your voice. My voice
is a whisper,
but it is learning
to whisper your name.

A Stubborn Kindness

In order to love you I must call to me every piece of fruit
that has been sliced and set in neat rows before me,

the fervent promises made in spring, the bed
licked clean by the tongue of the moon.

How you made my room a maze of light, closed
my eyes and placed the darkest chocolate on my tongue.

When I place my hand on your chest,
I call to me every time I was not allowed to apologize,

that evening the fireflies in the wet grass made me think
all I could be made of is light, and light,

the few nights my mother brought me tea in bed,
that one time she let me wipe her face dry.

How you kiss me as if my bones were branches
full with fruit for your taking.

How I yearn to love like rain, falling without measure.

What the Body Knows

To look in the mirror and let my hand drift
to all the places I can no longer hate.
In this quiet moment I must orphan the panic,
pull it out of me as a grape is pulled from its soft, wet peel.

This is the only sound of departure I have come to love.

She asks me in that quiet voice
What if love doesn't have to hurt?
What if it's not giving you all my salt to judge, then lick?
What if it's not undressing while turning my face away?

Mother once told me that love is all about forgetting.
What if it's the duty of daughters
to make themselves remember:
his lashes making lace of skin.
The hands too small to defend.
The men emboldened by the word *no*.

And also
how she gently wakes me by putting her hand, there.
How she washes apricots for me in the morning.
How she calls to me even when panic
takes me by the stem of my neck.

What my body knows is that this
is what it means to put a bird whole
onto my tongue,
feathers hanging over my lip

before I bite down and let her see
how a crack of bone
makes a wing
of my mouth.

UNSOLICITED ADVICE FOR THE QUEER ASIAN GIRLS JUST TRYING TO MAKE IT

after Jeanann Verlee

When your mother forces you out of the car, let her. When she tries to apologize years later for doing so, let her. When you're old enough to understand how mistakes can be well-intentioned, answer the phone. When she refers to your girlfriend as your roommate, plan on inviting her back for the next holiday. When she asks if the man you went to lunch with is your boyfriend, simply say *no*. When you want to let your anger swallow any body close or small enough, remember that change takes a long time. When she ignores your fiancé when making introductions, remember how at least she asks about her when she calls. When at your wedding, she sees you're both loved and belong, don't remind her of everything she's done before. When she finally tells your wife she loves her, let yourself cry, all the longing built from ten years of waiting. Let her see your tears, and try to forgive her, and yourself, for letting it take this long.

THE TREE TO THE SKY

I have readied myself for centuries
to offer this to you, and here you meet me
with rain to drink in small gulps
and frequent sips. I am almost, almost.
Soon I will shine without
turning my head down, open
my shirt to you, the wind, the birds.

CUT TO BLOOM

Flowers are the only things (*immagration*
we can cut from a body,   *reference?*)
put in water, and watch open.

Today the subway is blasted full
by bouquets smearing tongues
on cheeks and brushing buttons
to be pushed only in emergency.

The man in line in front of me
at the flower shop is now
on my train home.

Two dozen bouquets
he pays for with a shiny card,
almost dropping his coffee
in the exchange.
His calla lilies bumping along
to the bass notes of the F train
could be for the daughter
he's meeting for the first time.

Maybe he'll give her the lilies, say
You won't remember me,
but these flowers
have known how to love you
their entire lives.

        (family) business reference?
The irises are going to a widow
who is learning to cook at age fifty-two.
The alstroemerias are a tambourine
in the fists of a man whispering his words in practice.

The birds of paradise bounce
in the hands of the doctor
waiting all day to soak in his wife's river
and let her call him earth.

This one orchid is for my father
to say I relieve him of the hopes
he will become like the men in this poem,
and that no matter how rough the cut
there is a chance
for a bloom.

MEMORY IS A GENTLE BLESSING

so be careful.

For you the day at the park was proof
that emotions are the play things of men
but for him, it was just another Saturday afternoon.
You're allowed to say *no*. You're allowed
to think of yourself
over his ego.

You have been pretending for a long time
that you're like everyone else
so stop berating and pacing
and pleading to an empty sky.
No one is counting, but I'm sure
you've done your time.

Memory is a gentle blessing—
all you will forget
when you're standing at the altar
looking at her face,
the bruises belonging
to someone else by now

the names you were called
flecking off like old paint,
your mother's eyes
holding something new
and yes there's that time, and that one too
that makes you think that this goodness is a lie

but how else can you remember
that you deserve to stand here
if only because of all
the blood you have left behind

trying to be worthy
of wanting something
just because your tongue insists
on wrapping around its name.

ODE TO UNLEARNING

When a picture is all
you have, you remember

the way your father
held you easy
like sunlight in a window
or water in a cup,
the sides of his hair short
just like you
in the mirror now,
surprised to see his face
after all these years.

The biggest insult
Umma threw at you,
right after the cop lights,
the shelter, the divorce,
was to say *You are just like your appa*,
leaving your socks around the house
like an untrained dog
unsure of what to claim
so claiming everything.

When I first called
my father-in-law *Dad*
I had rehearsed it a million times,
wanting to sound casual enough
everyone would know I was ready

the word finally untied
from bruise and ache and *if only*

and brandishing it now
like a key to the room
where *father* means a stiff drink
but not a stiff hand, a hug
that is tender but not

an apology, a man
who can hold you
without falling apart.

I am not my appa
I say to the face with the new haircut
and the mirror remembers what forgiving him
felt like, wrenching it out like an inch of glass,
him free, and I too

no more wondering
what I could have done
to hide the soju and the rum
or keep my mother's jaw
from his fists

but here he is in the mirror,
looking like the picture of him
in '89 at the ocean
and it's the only one
of us together, smiling

and the only task left
is to remember
I got from him
what I needed.

Split to Shape

In our first year of marriage
I couldn't stop testing for cracks.
Children who raise other children
learn that nothing is certain:
food can come out of a box,
a bin, a welt. Rules can be a fist,
not enough, too much. Children
can be an excuse, a ruse, a sore.

Because I was both
an excuse and a sore
I can forgive my mother now,

my degrees paid for in full,
my younger sister saved
from memories of a father
she never met, Mother's
desperate years only
a story she knows.

In a house full of children
holding keys, the only rule
is to not become like the one
with the fist, the monster
under the bed, Father gone
but not what he has caused
so my wife knows the monster too well:

Be perfect it says, a picture of order and habit
because who in their right mind
could divorce perfect.
Cook meals for the whole week
on Sundays, plan all weekends
for the month in advance, and also:
assume her disappointment
means her disappearance, a raised tone,
a smack, and while my wife retreats

to the other room, I'm trying to remember
that this is my house and my choice,
my fist, my rules to be thrown
like a brick against the thick
incessant dark
but how quickly my body raises
the alarm, remembers
the formulas from childhood and yet

here is my wife pulling me out
of my curl on the couch, here
are her strong hands willing me back
to our Brooklyn apartment,
here in the morning
with my cup of coffee.

Most days, it is hard to remember
I am worthy to be loved, even without
the right answer, the right joke,
the right moment.

And yet, here is my wife,
trying to tell me
a story around her toothbrush,
bragging about me to her parents,
bringing my favorite dessert home, as if
I could still be an unpredictable ending
that she wants to see unfold.

Rest in Peace
Moon Sung Choi
1955-2019

GLOSSARY: IN ORDER OF APPEARANCE

한: *Han*
> While being a notoriously hard word to translate, *han* includes the idea of a shared struggle and inheritance that is a part of the Korean personality and cultural make-up. The word includes notions of injustice, grief, sorrow, and trauma while also encompassing the resilience of the Korean people to survive an intense history of colonial rule, fracture, and violence. Sometimes the word is said to convey the strength to endure without drawing attention to the struggle as a matter of pride and propriety.

Umma: *Um mah*
> Mama

Appa: *A pah*
> Father

Halmoni: *Hal mon ee*
> Paternal grandmother

애들: *Ae deul*
> Children

식혜: *Shik hye*
> A delicious Korean rice drink

만두: *Mandu*
> Dumplings

떡국: *Tteok guk*
> Korean rice cake soup. Often eaten on New Year's Day and special holidays as rice symbolizes bounty and luck.

갈비: *Kalbi*
> Korean short rib barbeque

몸조심해: *Moem jo shim hye*
> A phrase that means "take care of yourself."

아름아: *Arhm-ah*
   The suffix *ah* is often attached to names as a term of endearment.

예쁘다: *Ye peu da*
   Pretty

아름답다: *A reum dap da*
   Beautiful

가을: *Ga eul*
   Autumn

언니: *Unni*
   The older "sister" of a female speaker. This term of respect can be applied to any woman who is older than the speaker.

오빠: *Oppa*
   The older "brother" of a female speaker. This term of respect can be applied to any man who is older than the speaker.

ACKNOWLEDGMENTS

Thank you to the editors of the following publications for publishing poems from this collection, sometimes in different forms: *Barrow Street*, *Daring to Repair Anthology* by Wising Up Press, *Foglifter*, *F(r)iction*, *Lantern Review*, *Lumina*, *Massachusetts Review*, *Otoliths*, *Peal*, *Queer Anthology of Literatures*, *Scholars & Rogues Literary Journal*, *Split this Rock*, *Track/Four*, and *Two Hawks Quarterly*. Thank you to Write Bloody for believing in these poems and taking a chance on me.

Thank you to my family, Myung Choi, Maureen Choi, and Elizabeth/ Baby/Bo Choi, for trusting me with your stories and for believing in the transformative power of articulating them. You have helped me become strong and fierce, and turn the challenges of our lives into some of our greatest strengths. I am so proud of the ways we've refused to succumb to trauma. Thank you for dreaming up a life beyond survival with me.

Thank you to my wife, A.M. Wild, who not only helped me come up with the title of this book after reading and editing the manuscript several times over but also took on the cleaning/cooking/dog walking so I would have time to dedicate to this project. You grounded me in bravery and its necessity when I was scared to claim my full self, and believed in these poems from the very beginning when we sat across from each other at Sarah Lawrence. This book wouldn't be possible without your meticulous and expansive edits, and your ability to guide people to the truest versions of themselves.

Thank you to my in-laws for welcoming me in and loving me like one of your own: Mario Carrillo, Jody Lounsbury, Gregg Lounsbury, Lindsay DeWitt, AJ DeWitt, Andi DeWitt, Jacqueline DeWitt, Meghan Lee, Matthew Lee, Olivia Lee, Camden Lee, and all my other wonderful in-laws. You fill my life with so much love and joy.

Thank you to the wonderful folks who edited and read my poems, sometimes many times over, and always with your brilliance and generosity: Maggie Ambrosino-Sands, Chelsea Bayouth, Derrick C. Brown, Adam Falkner, Winona León, Heidi Andrea Restrepo Rhodes, Jon Sands, Sun Yung Shin, R.A. Villanueva, and Annie

Virginia. Thank you to Zoe Norvell for creating a beautiful and perfect cover for this book. Thank you to Cathy Park Hong, Phil Kaye, Pat Rosal, and Jeanann Verlee for writing the blurbs and your encouragement and love at such a critical moment.

Thank you to my Kundiman fam for helping me contend with the hyphen in my Asian-American identity with love and possibility, and helping me see that there doesn't need to be a cost to my belonging. Thank you, too, for the amazing doors you have opened for me. All of my accomplishments are peppered with your support.

Thank you to my incredible teachers who put the shovel, the microscope, the pen into my hands. Thank you especially to Jeff Kass, my first creative writing teacher, who changed the entire landscape of my life and showed me that writing can be a way to forge my own compass. You have made all the difference. Thank you to Cathy Park Hong, who asked me the exact questions about identity I needed to stay true to the purpose of this book. Thank you to Patrick Rosal, whose classes make a church of poems, and to all the other teachers who helped this book evolve and claim itself.

Thank you to my therapist whose generosity has allowed me to do much of the work that was needed to write these poems. I wish that therapy was more integrated into all of our lives instead of being a privilege just for the few.

Thank you to Sy Klipsch-Abudu, who filmed my video for the Write Bloody semi-finalist round, and who took my author photo. You are and will always be an essential member of my dream team. Thank you to Sy's amazing wife, Kait Klipsch-Abudu, for the most nonjudgmental love I have ever experienced, and your amazing gluten-free cookies. Thank you to Zoe Maya Jones for being my forever lighthouse, and for feeding me in all the ways that matter. Thank you to Maggie Bragagnolo for being my sister since our days at Pioneer and all the ways you've shown up for me and my family.

Thank you to my tribe, my chosen fam, for infusing my life with your light, even when I am only a fledgling and finding my way. Your love has allowed me to shine, to name and love myself: Nya Abudu, Coert Ambrosino, Merrin Clough, Marcie Grambeau, Danielle Hartounian,

Paige Heron, Michael Moliterno, Jordan Peschke, Chelsea Rhodes, Jake Salt, Hayley Schmidt, and Hannah Swihart.

Thank you to everyone who has believed in me, especially to Barbara Reese for supporting my ability to attend the MFA program at Sarah Lawrence. Thank you to all the Neutral Zone fam, the Pioneer parking lot troublemakers, the Warren Wilson crew, the NYC community of poets, and my colleagues at the Ethical Culture Fieldston School.

Thank you to the workshops that helped me carve out space to write and provided such fertile ground: In Real Life, VONA Across the Country, R.A. Villanueva's New Chords workshop, and of course, Kundiman.

Thank you to AWP, Split this Rock, the Adirondack Center for Writing, and the Dialogue Arts Project for inviting me to speak on panels or teach with you, affording different venues to keep this love alive and pushing me to extend and improve my craft.

Last but not least, thank you, dear reader, for letting this book accompany you for a while. I hope it helps you believe a little more in the transformative power of articulating our stories, feel a little more seen, a little less in the margins, and that there is a space where you too, can claim your story.

ABOUT THE AUTHOR

ARHM CHOI WILD is a queer, Korean-American poet who grew up in the slam community of Ann Arbor, Michigan, and went on to perform across the country, including at Brave New Voices, the New York City Poetry Festival, and Asheville Wordfest. Arhm is a Kundiman fellow with an MFA in Poetry from Sarah Lawrence College, and was a finalist for the Jake Adam York Prize in 2019. Their work has been anthologized in *Daring to Repair* by Wising Up Press and *The Queer Movement Anthology of Literatures*, and appears in *Barrow Street*, *The Massachusetts Review*, *Split this Rock*, *Foglifter*, *Lantern Review*, *F(r)iction*, and other publications. They work as the Director of the Progressive Teaching Institute and as a Diversity Coordinator at a school in New York City.

arhmchoiwild.com

IF YOU LIKE ARHM CHOI WILD, ARHM LIKES...

Amulet
Jason Bayani

Drive Here and Devastate Me
Megan Falley

The Madness Vase
Andrea Gibson

Rise of the Trust Fall
Mindy Nettifee

This Way to the Sugar
Hieu Minh Nguyen

Racing Hummingbirds
Jeanann Verlee

Write Bloody Publishing publishes and promotes great books of poetry every year. We believe that poetry can change the world for the better. We are an independent press dedicated to quality literature and book design, with an office in Los Angeles, California.

We are grassroots, DIY, bootstrap believers. Pull up a good book and join the family. Support independent authors, artists, and presses.

Want to know more about Write Bloody books, authors, and events? Join our mailing list at

www.writebloody.com

WRITE BLOODY BOOKS

CPSIA information can be obtained
at www.ICGtesting.com
Printed in the USA
FSHW011916030720
71764FS